CHAINS OF WISDOM

Compiled by Jan Barnes

MORE HAND-ME-DOWN WISDOM

Copper Beech Publishing

First Published in Great Britain 1991 by
Copper Beech Publishing Ltd
East Grinstead, Sussex RH19 4HF
© Copyright Jan Barnes 1991

ISBN 0 9516295 3 0

A CIP catalogue record for this book is available
from the British Library.

Acknowledgements are on page 64.

Cover design, French & Galbally, Tunbridge Wells.
Printed in Great Britain by
Hillman Printers, Frome.

Introduction

...there are a hundred things one has to know...I mean passwords, and signs, and sayings which have power and effect, and plants you carry in your pocket, and verses you repeat...

Kenneth Grahame wrote The Wind in the Willows in 1908, and even now it contains some of the first 'passwords and signs and sayings' many people memorise.

Years later, another 'saying' heard on a radio programme was enough incentive for me to begin my collection of treasured words.

It seems most of us have a cache of words – fragments from another time, penned in a diary, framed on a wall, or just engraved in the mind after a conversation.

Are we in danger of losing this link?

Take the romantic notion of the front porch swing – the sitting out in the evening, having time to talk to each other, read books, pass the time of day with the neighbours out for their evening stroll.

Have we sacrificed this kind of everyday contact in our frantic efforts to 'always be in touch'?

Hand-me-down Wisdom was the first collection of those threads of wisdom which link one generation with another. Now, Chains of Wisdom, a second set of people offer the opportunity to discover some of their treasured words (or, not so treasured – see Keith Waterhouse!).

Some of the other 'links' in these Chains of Wisdom are made by words quoted or read from the pages of a book. Also included is a collection of maxims and sayings collected from autograph books. The thoughts and wisdom of past generations always make good reading. (Anyone who has read Hand-me-down Wisdom will remember the actor Derek Nimmo quoting from his autograph book two sayings from his grandmother).

...why do some phrases linger and not others......some books reach out and speak so clearly?

Do we have a sense which recognises the answer to some future soul-need, or is there no such thing as wisdom at all — just words allowing us access to our own answers?

It seems our personal treasure chest of words can be called on at random throughout life…added to without our realising as we talk to an old friend, a stranger, listen to a teacher or parent, watch a play or read a book…..

poets and songwriters were the original messengers, but other live performances, to smaller audiences, are performed daily by those perhaps unaware of the long-lasting effect of their words

….this book will leave you wondering about your own chains of wisdom, left behind on your life's travels — advice and greetings card words; autograph book messages and live performances…..sayings which can have power and effect.

Jan Barnes

Paddy Ashdown

Member of Parliament, Yeovil, Leader Liberal Democrats

This is the nearest thing to a piece of contemporary folk wisdom I can offer. It comes from The Gulag Archipelago by Solzhenitsen.

If you want I'll spell it out for you right now. Do not pursue what is illusory — property and position: all that is gained at the expense of your nerves decade after decade and is confiscated in one fell night. Live with a steady superiority over life — don't be afraid of misfortune and do not yearn after happiness; it is, after all, the same: the bitter doesn't last forever and the sweet never fills the cup to overflowing. It is enough if you don't freeze in the cold and if thirst and hunger don't claw at your insides. If your back isn't broken, if your feet can walk, if both arms can bend, if both eyes see, and if both ears hear, then whom should you envy? And why? Our envy of others devours us most of all. Rub your eyes and purify your heart — and prize above all else in the world those who love you and who wish you well.

Pam Ayres

Writer

This on being the mother of teenage children!

Oh, to be half as wonderful as my children thought I was <u>once</u>...and only half as stupid as they think I am <u>now</u>

Bryan Gould

Member of Parliament, Dagenham

This remark was made to me by a friend (Annie Long, wife of James Long, former economics correspondent of the BBC), some time ago in relation to life in general.

I often remind myself of this when in the middle of an extremely busy life I might otherwise ignore moments of enjoyment or relaxation or pleasure.

This is not a dress rehearsal,
this is the real thing

Laurie Lee MBE

Poet and Author

I can remember no 'inherited wisdom'
except perhaps the occasion when my mother,
walking back from Stroud in the driving rain,
is passed by a rich plump farmer in his horse
and trap and mutters – half to herself – this
ancient cry.

"You know, I could have married that man, if only I'd played my cards right"

Cardew Robinson

Actor/Writer/Broadcaster

A friend sent me a short story about a love affair set in Japan which quoted this Japanese proverb. This stuck in my mind for a long time...and one day I sat down and wrote the lyric 'The First Hello the Last Goodbye'. Roger Whitaker put the music to it and it has thrilled me to hear that warm singer using my words from the original Japanese inspiration.

The first Hello to a new person is the beginning
of the last Goodbye to the same person

Ernie Wise

Comedian

These words of wisdom came from my mother.

This saying was my father's.

When there is no money in the house,
love flies out of the window

Your best friend is your bank book

Spend a little and save a little

If there is no argument in the house,
it means there is an underdog somewhere

ENDEAVOUR NOT TO HAVE
      CHAMPAGNE TASTES
ON A BROWN ALE
            INCOME

Put your feet up
        whenever you can
Life will send you plenty
      of standing to do

Whatever you can, or dream
you can, begin it.
Boldness has power
and magic in it

Be careful what you set your heart upon
for you will surely get it.

S*ir Richard Attenborough* CBE

Actor/Producer/Director

When I was first given the Louis Fischer biography of Mahatma Ghandi I read this passage which instantly convinced me that this was a subject that I was to make into a film.

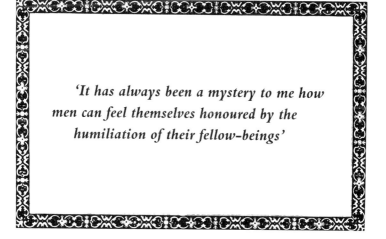

'It has always been a mystery to me how
men can feel themselves honoured by the
humiliation of their fellow-beings'

Tony Benn

Member of Parliament, Chesterfield

Reinhold Niebuhr – who was a distinguished American theologian and a family friend.

Man's capacity for evil makes democracy necessary,
man's capacity for good makes democracy possible

Roy Hudd

Comedian/Actor/Writer

This is the one phrase I have before me on my desk and it was coined by the film producer Mike Todd.

Have success
and there will always be fools
to say you have talent

Jean Rook

Assistant Editor and Chief Columnist,
Daily Express

These words were from my father – a Lincolnshire man – he always used to tell me this – it was probably his own philosophy.

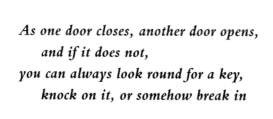

As one door closes, another door opens,
and if it does not,
you can always look round for a key,
knock on it, or somehow break in

V*alerie Singleton*

Broadcaster

I do have a quote I like very much which comes from E.M. Forster's 'A Passage to India'.

*'Life never gives us what we want at the
moment that we consider appropriate.
Adventures do occur, but not punctually'*

A*lan Sugar*

Chairman and Managing Director, Amstrad plc

One of the first lessons I learnt in business was taught to me by my first boss. He told me I believed too much in my advisers. It is true to say that in the early stages....having advisers was very useful.

But as time went by, I started to realise that I was able to make moves and innovate in the city in a way that they had never seen. It's the old lesson of taking over from the professor. He can lay down the basics and it's up to you to absorb and then go on in your own special way, enhance and **add your own special touch**.

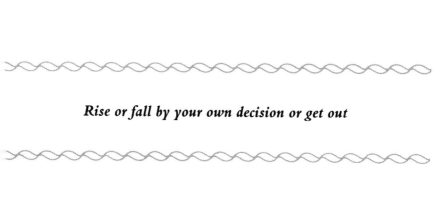

Rise or fall by your own decision or get out

Norman Wisdom

Actor/Comedian

These words were passed on to me by my mother when I was a child. The word 'gay' has an entirely different connotation these days, but my dear mother meant it 'just happy.'

He's lucky who's plucky
He's happy who's gay
He's wealthy who's healthy
So wise folk say

Celebrate Life:—
for time is always more
advanced than you would think

MEMO

Look out
not in,

Look forward
not back.

Fix your mind on each step

As you take it

And none will seem

harder to take

than another

Do not squander time
Such is the stuff life
is made of

Arthur R Ashe Jr

Professional Lawn Tennis Player

Henry David Thoreau, Man against the state, 'Civil Disobedience'.

'It is not a man's duty, as a matter of course, to devote himself to the eradication of any, even the most enormous wrong...but it is his duty, at least, to wash his hands of it, and if he gives it no thought longer, <u>not</u> to give it practically his support'

John Osborne

Playwright

Kipling – this is probably my first choice as 'something I wish I'd written'. It is a small miriade of terseness and wisdom, containing that sublime gift of irony that is special to the English language. It also sends tooth and claw feminists screaming from the room!

A woman is only a woman
but a good cigar is a smoke

Chris Patten

Member of Parliament, Bath

My father used to say that one should always leave the stage while the audience is still clapping.

I hope this is a piece of wisdom which I will recall when in due course I need to do so!

Always leave the stage
while the audience is still clapping

Harold Prince

Theatre Director/Producer

Many years ago, when I was apprenticing to George Abbott, the dean of American directors, I watched him struggling with the problems of a particular production. On an evening when the play did not go well we went, as we usually did, for a bowl of corn flakes and a glass of milk. When I asked him why he wasn't anguishing as I was, he replied with the following: 'If you want a long life in the theatre and you're struggling with a particular project, remind yourself that it's only a show and there's another one where that came from'.

Fifty projects later, it has stood me in good stead.

*..it's only a show and there's
ther one where that came from.*

A*thene Seyler**

These are the words my father Clarence
Seyler always said to me when I was young.

Be good and let who will be clever

Do noble deeds not dream them all the day long

Arnold Wesker

Playwright/Director

These are not the exact words, only more or less, from Thornton Wilder's novel 'The Bridge of San Luis Rey'.

Words which reconcile rather than words of wisdom.

*'Of two people who love,
one loves the least'*

Katharine Whitehorn

Journalist

My mother used to urge us to consider anybody we might be thinking of marrying not only in terms of 'that man and no other', but 'that life and no other' which seemed to me extremely sound.

We have tried diligently to teach our boys the poker maxim 'never draw to an inside straight', though we were distressed to hear that the younger one has been through Las Vegas and found a form of poker in which it is legitimate to draw to an inside straight.

that life and no other

Never draw to an inside straight

Stay Strong
Stay Happy

Treasure friendship above all
tis someone to catch
lest the other should fall

ESTERDAY is A CANCELLED CHEQUE
TOMORROW is AN I.O.U.
TODAY IS READY CASH
USE IT

its not what you do
that counts
but what you are
that counts

S*ir Alec Guinness* CBE

Actor

This quotation from 'Hamlet' (Act 5) has been most useful in life.

'The readiness is all'

Mary Peters

Olympic gold medallist 1972

Dad always quoted this to me as I grew up. I think the poem speaks for itself.

PERHAPS NOT SURPRISINGLY,
THESE MOTIVATIONAL WORDS WERE
ALSO CONTRIBUTED BY:

Arnold Palmer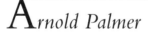

Golf Professional

If you think you are beaten, you are
If you think you dare not, you don't
If you'd like to win, but think you can't
It's almost certain you won't.
If you think you'll lose, you've lost
For out of the world we find
Success begins with a fellow's will –
It's all in the state of mind.
If you think you're outclassed you are
You've got to think high to rise
You've got to be sure of yourself before
You can ever win a prize.
Life's battles don't always go
To the stronger or faster man
But sooner or later the man who wins
Is the one who Thinks he can.

William *Stafford*

Poet

My father gave me the best guidance when I was young. And I remember particularly one walk we had together – his guidance and wisdom came as a combination of action and words, and I put it down in the poem 'A Walk with My Father When I Was Eight'. This is the way it begins:

Here is a space for the way the day started:
(————)
Here is a word for the sun: (————)
I can't fill these blanks for sure any more:
that day we were both young

Keith *Waterhouse*

Writer

The only bit of wisdom I know is Montaigne's 'All permanent decisions are made in a temporary frame of mind', which I read when I was about eighteen. But I am afraid I have rarely heeded it.

*All permanent decisions
are made in a
temporary frame of mind*

Lord Wilson of Rievaulx
KG OBE FRS

Former Prime Minister

My father was fond of and often quoted to me both in my schooldays and throughout my early career, the words from the Gettysburg address.

I felt strongly then, and feel so even to this day, that this is what politics is all about and we forget it at our peril.

work they have thus far so nobly advanced. It is rather for us to be here dedicated to the great task remaining before us, that from these honoured dead we take increased devotion to that cause for which they here gave the last full measure of devotion; that we here highly resolve that the dead shall not have died in vain, that this nation, under God, shall have a new birth of freedom; and that government of the people, by the people, and for the people, shall not perish from the earth.

Gettysburg, 19 Nov 1863

Acknowledgements

The author would like to thank these contributors for finding the time to share their chains of wisdom.

We gratefully acknowledge the permission granted to reprint extracts from the following authors, publishers and authors' representatives.

Extract from Mahatma Ghandi Biography by Louis Fischer by kind permission of the publishers Jonathan Cape.

The Bridge of San Luis Rey by Thornton Wilder, published by Penguin Books. Full correct quotation 'Even in the most perfect love, one person loves less profoundly than the other'

Extract from 'A Passage to India' by kind permission of Kings College Cambridge and The Society of Authors as the literary representatives of the E.M. Forster estate.

Extract from The Gulag Archipalago by Alexander Solzhenitsyn by kind permission of the Publishers Harvill.

'A Walk With My Father When I Was Eight' from 'Smoke's Way', William Stafford, Graywolf Press, Minnesota.

Every effort has been made to trace ownership of the quotations used in this anthology. If any omission has occurred it is inadvertent and it should be brought to the attention of the publishers.

Also available, containing more fragments from another time,
collected from Joan Baez, David Bellamy, Henry Cooper,
Derek Nimmo, Margaret Thatcher…and more.

HAND-ME-DOWN
WISDOM

A BOOK OF TREASURED WORDS